Contents

Parsley	6
Basil	8
Nutmeg and Mace	10
Pepper	12
Saffron	14
Cinnamon	16
Coriander	18
Chamomile	20
Mustard	22
Thyme	24
Spearmint	26
Other herbs and spices	28

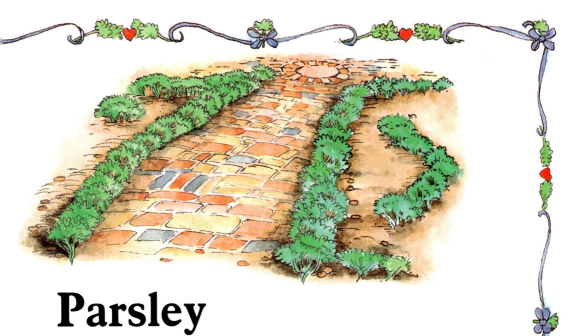

Parsley

Parsley is one of the best known herbs. It first grew in warm countries like Greece and Turkey and was brought to Britain by the Romans.

There are many different kinds of parsley but all parsley grows as a thick clump of feathery green leaves in the first year. In the second year it has a yellowy green flowering stem about one metre high.

Parsley is rich in vitamins. Chopped up small it is used to give a lovely flavour to soups and stews. Parsley sauce is traditionally served with fish.

Basil

Basil grows best where it is hot and dry. It first grew in India and then spread through Asia to Europe. It reached Britain in the sixteenth century.

Basil has purpley white flowers in midsummer and juicy, broad leaves. It grows to about 50 centimetres tall.

In Italy, basil leaves are chopped up very small to make pesto, a special sauce that is often served with pasta. They are also used to give a delicious sharp flavour to salads. Basil leaves are a strong tonic and good for settling upset stomachs.

There are many different kinds of basil including Dark Opal, which is a distinctive purple colour.

Nutmeg and Mace

Nutmeg and mace both come from the fruit of the nutmeg tree. Nutmeg trees grow in the Caribbean and other tropical countries. They have smooth, grcy bark and dark green leaves.
    The fruit has a yellow skin and looks rather

like a small apple. Inside the fruit is the nutmeg and the mace.

The mace is a bright red waxy net that protects the nutmeg.

The nutmeg and mace are dried separately before being used as flavourings for sweet or savoury dishes.

Pepper

Pepper comes from berries which start green and turn orange and red when they ripen.

Pepper berries come from a vine that grows to about six metres up trees in hot forests of India, Asia and the Caribbean.

Some berries are picked unripe and left in the sun until they are dry and black. They are black pepper corns.

Other berries are left to ripen on the vine. When they are picked the coloured outside is stripped off and the pale inner core is dried. These are white pepper corns.

Pepper has always been an important flavouring. It was once so valuable that it was used instead of money.

Saffron

Saffron is a kind of crocus. It has purple or blue flowers. Inside the flowers there are bright orange stigmas which are visible when the flowers are fully open. Saffron was first grown in Turkey. Now it comes from many places and especially from Spain where the best saffron is grown.

Saffron is expensive because 70,000 to 80,000 stigmas are needed for each 500 grams of saffron and every stigma must be picked by hand! Luckily, only a tiny amount is needed to colour food a beautiful orangey yellow and give it a slightly spicey flavour.

Saffron is used in rice dishes such as Spanish paella and Indian curry. In Cornwall, it is used to make saffron cake which is a distinctive yellow colour.

Cinnamon

Cinnamon trees have yellowish white flowers, dark blue berries and tough, shiny leaves. They grow in the Caribbean, Sri Lanka, and other Eastern countries. The spice called cinnamon comes from the bark of the tree. The bark is stripped off the trees and then left to dry. It curls up into quills as it dries.

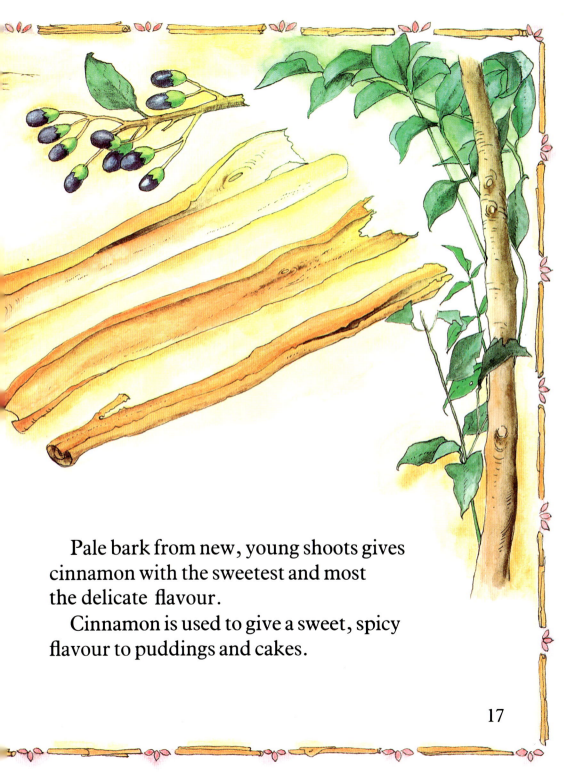

Pale bark from new, young shoots gives cinnamon with the sweetest and most the delicate flavour.

Cinnamon is used to give a sweet, spicy flavour to puddings and cakes.

Coriander

Ripe coriander seeds have a strong and delicious smell and give a sweet, slightly bitter flavour. They can be used as a flavouring for sweet or savoury foods. Fresh coriander leaves are often used whole to flavour curries and salads.

Coriander plants grow to about 60 centimetres tall and have pinkish flowers which are followed later in the year by large, round seeds.

They have been grown and used in India, China and Egypt for thousands of years.

Chamomile

Chamomile grows all over Europe. It has flowers with yellow centres surrounded by white rays.

Wild chamomile flowers can be dried and used to make a soothing tea which is thought to be good for the stomach. They can also be squeezed to produce a strong smelling oil which works well as a hair conditioner. It can even be used to make blonde hair blonder!

Mustard

Mustard has a hot, strong flavour and is used – in small amounts – with savoury dishes. Black mustard comes from the seeds of a plant which grows to about 1·5 metres tall. It is common in many parts of the world. The plant has yellow flowers and smooth seed pods which contain reddish brown seeds. The pods are picked and crushed to produce a powder which is mixed with water or vinegar to produce an oily paste. This is the mustard we eat.

Mustard can be added to baths, especially for soothing tired feet.

Thyme

Thyme grows as a spreading bush only about 30 centimetres above the ground. It has grey-green leaves and small white or purpley flowers. Thyme can grow on stony ground where it is warm and sunny. It has a delicious strong smell when the sun shines on it.

There are several different sorts of thyme, including wild thyme, garden thyme and lemon thyme.

The leaves of garden thyme are picked and dried for use in cooking soups and stews.

The leaves of wild thyme can be squeezed out to produce thymol, an oil which helps heal cuts and aids digestion. The Romans believed that a bath in thyme water would give them courage.

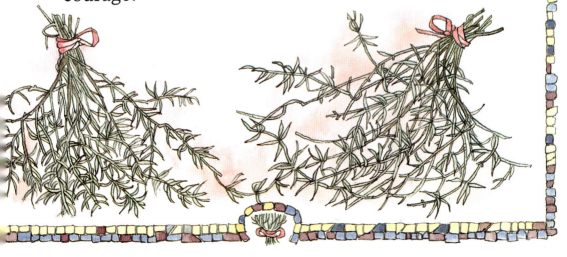

Spearmint

There are many different kinds of mint and all of them have broad green leaves which give the flavour.

In Britain spearmint is used to make mint sauce to go with lamb.

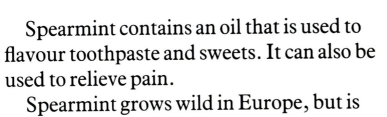

Spearmint contains an oil that is used to flavour toothpaste and sweets. It can also be used to relieve pain.

Spearmint grows wild in Europe, but is usually found in gardens. It grows in a spike with green leaves and pale lilac flowers.

There are many different herbs and spices and some are shown in this picture. Many of them are dried to preserve them. See how many you can find in your local store or supermarket.

Bergamot

Borage

Tansy

Fennel

Oregano

Sesame

Lemon Balm

Bay

Poppy Seed

Feverfew

28

Tarragon

Rosemary

Sage

Lavender

Garlic

Allspice

Chilli

Cardamon

Cloves

Ginger

Aniseed

Cumin

Star Anise